ALEX'S
Adventures
in the Country

Eduard Delgado ★ Francesc Rovira

Derrydale Books
New York

"Look! Chip has found a rabbit track."

2

When summer comes, Alex and his friends think up all kinds of games. But not everyone in the town is on vacation.

So many different things are going on around Alex! But he sees only the four-legged boat that keeps coming closer.

"Rosie, get out of the water! You don't know how to swim!"

4

"Cow ahead!"

5

"And we'll have a big sign saying
ALEX—PLANTS AND ANIMALS."

6

Alex and his friends go into town
riding behind the tractor. They have
decided to go to the country fair with
some of their treasures.

"Who's going to buy these birds' nests that came down in the rain?"

"These fish will be the best in the whole fair!"

"Chip will watch our stand."

"If we train him well, maybe the rabbit can learn to count."

9

"And later, we'll put on a puppet show."

10

But things are starting to get a bit mixed up. The squirrel has smelled chickens in the bag and with one leap he tears it open.

11

12

Little by little, the town square starts to fill up with strange things. There is an inventor up in the bell tower, a man keeps losing his rabbits and chickens, and a cow is bathing in the fountain.

'Come and see our show! Drawings, fish, and the wise squirrel!"

The fair is now very busy. People are selling vegetables and pottery, eggs and chickens, fish and odds and ends. Alex sells his drawings and the inventor explains how his mechanical wings work.

"Baa, baa, baa...."

16

"Hurray for Billy! Hurray for the little cowhand! Hurray!"

Rosie has won First Prize. The little cowhand deserves to have his picture in the newspaper but everyone will end up in it, looking very happy.

Alex and his friends put on a puppet show
while the townspeople have supper and
dance.

ALEX'S FIVE GAMES IN THE COUNTRY

1. ALEX'S GAME WITH THE ANIMALS

In this story there are 5 kinds of animals that appear in the pictures. See if you know what they are.

2. ALEX'S GAME WITH HIS "ZOO"

Alex likes to count, picture by picture, all the animals that appear in the story. Why don't you help him and write down the numbers in each spoke of this wheel?

3. ALEX'S GAME WITH HIS 5 DRAWINGS

Make a drawing in which Alex and the other characters in the story do different things with a broom, a rope, a ball, a hen, and a cat.

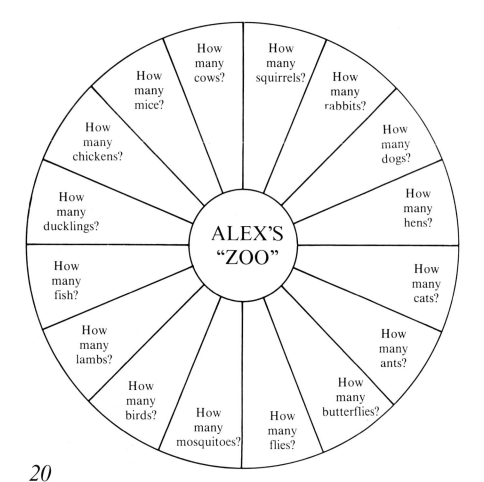

How many cows?
How many squirrels?
How many mice?
How many rabbits?
How many chickens?
How many dogs?
How many ducklings?
How many hens?
How many fish?
ALEX'S "ZOO"
How many cats?
How many lambs?
How many ants?
How many birds?
How many butterflies?
How many mosquitoes?
How many flies?